BRICK STI

PATTERNS

by Natalee Alex

24 SEED BEAD EARRINGS FRINGE

BEADING PATTERNS

Copyright © 2021 by Natalee Alex

Hi my dear friends!
My name is Natalee Alex.

I am very glad that you liked my patterns.
I hope you get a great jewelry.

So, for work you need Miyuki Delika
or Toho seed beads size 10/0, 11/0
or Czech seed beads size 10/0.

This picture shows the method
of weaving Bricks Stitch.

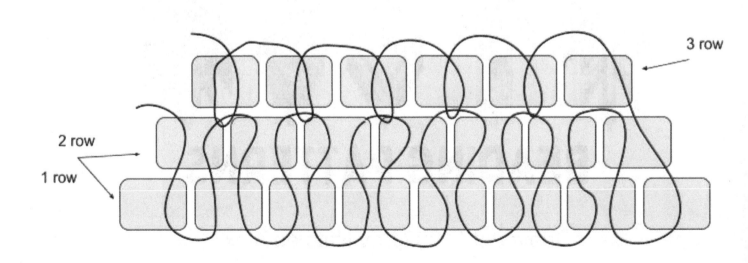

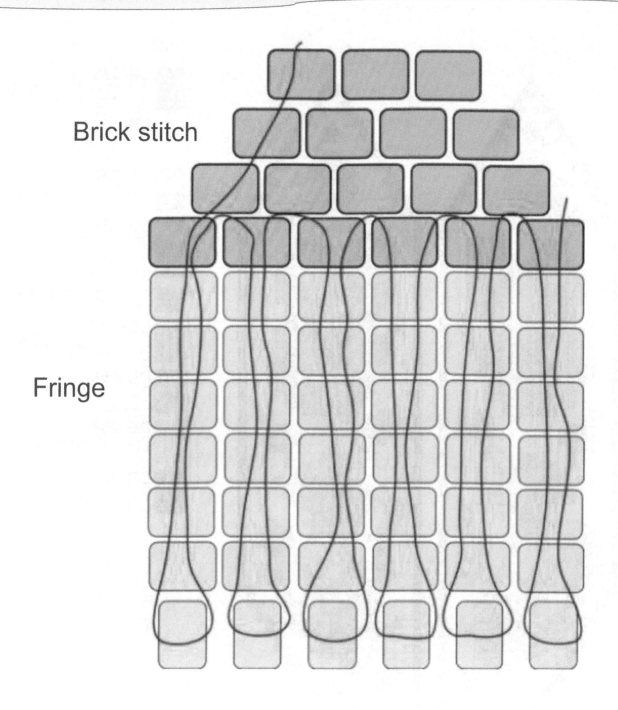

Brick stitch

Fringe

Wish you success.
If you have any questions my e-mail:
nataloka6699@gmail.com
Instagram @nataleealexdiy

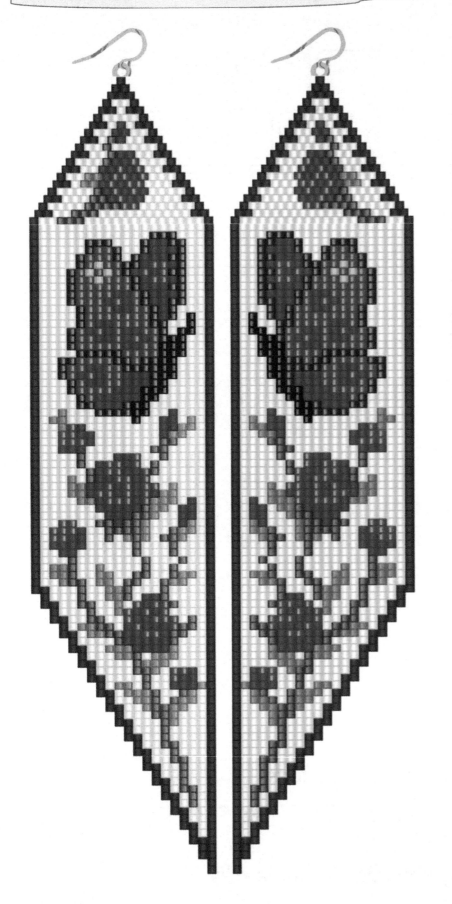

Bead List

■	**DB-378** Matte Metallic Brick Red Count: 248	
□	**DB-50** Crystal Luster Count: 686	
■	**DB-655** Opaque Kelly Green Count: 90	
■	**DB-159** Opaque Vermillion Red AB Count: 163	
■	**DB-103** Dark Topaz Rainbow Gold Count: 83	
■	**DB-796** Frosted Opaque Red Count: 172	
■	**DB-656** Opaque Green Count: 115	
□	**DB-658** Opaque Turquoise Green Count: 4	
■	**DB-10** Black Count: 29	

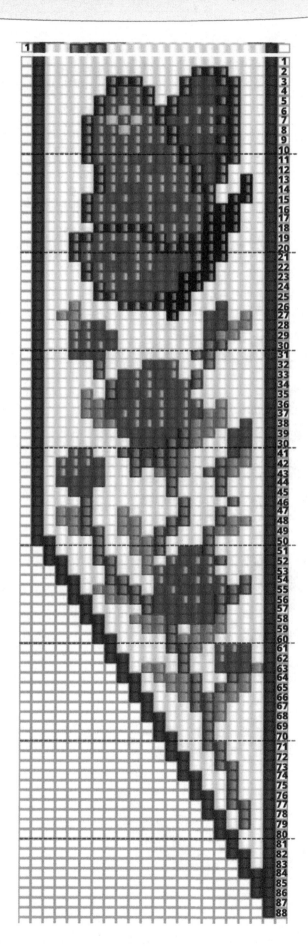

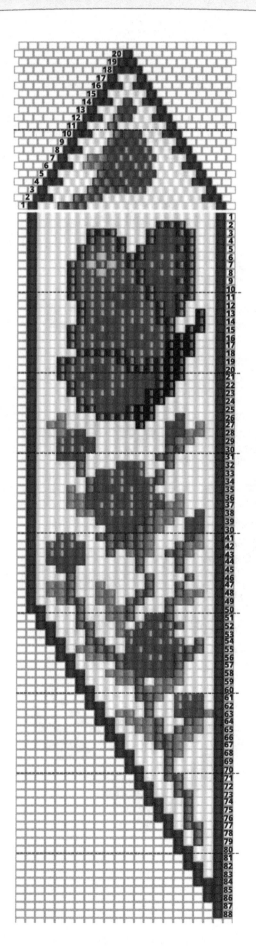

Bead List

	DB-50	Crystal Luster	Count: 642
	DB-77	Blue Lined Crystal AB	Count: 220
	DB-753	Matte Opaque Red	Count: 336
	DB-2	Metallic Dark Blue AB	Count: 92
	DB-113	Transparent Blue Luster	Count: 70

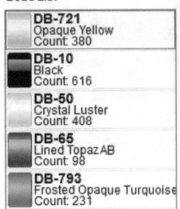

Bead List

DB-721
Opaque Yellow
Count: 380

DB-10
Black
Count: 616

DB-50
Crystal Luster
Count: 408

DB-65
Lined Topaz AB
Count: 98

DB-793
Frosted Opaque Turquoise
Count: 231

Bead List

	DB-851	Matte Crystal AB Count: 977
	DB-105	Garnet Gold Luster Count: 85
	DB-734	Opaque Chocolate Count: 304
	DB-778	Frosted Transparent Dark Count: 55
	DB-776	Frosted Transparent Emer Count: 68
	DB-62	Light Cranberry Lined Topa Count: 55

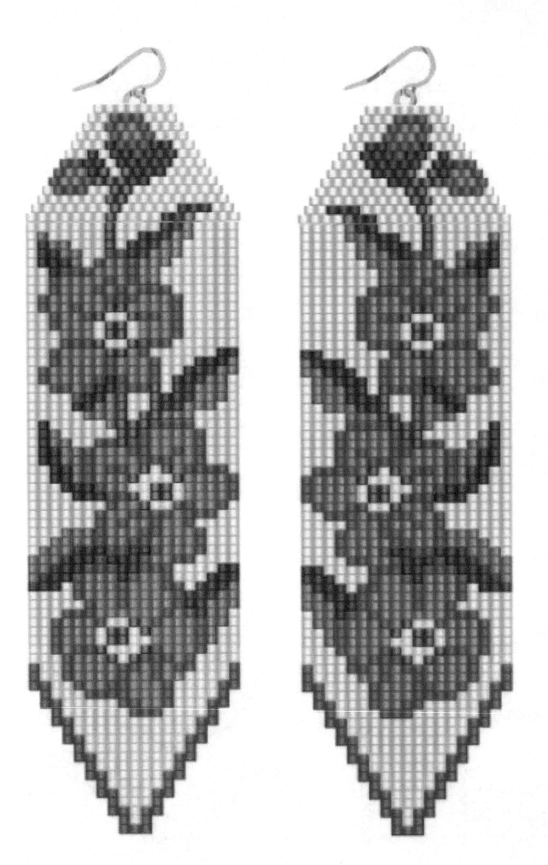

Bead List

DB-1673
Pearl Lined Pink AB
Count: 469

DB-778
Frosted Transparent Dark
Count: 265

DB-1807
Rose Satin
Count: 154

DB-797
Frosted Opaque Jade Gree
Count: 121

DB-460
Galvanized Cinnamon Brow
Count: 59

DB-724
Opaque Green
Count: 82

DB-1338
Silver Lined Rose
Count: 80

DB-751
Matte Opaque Yellow
Count: 68

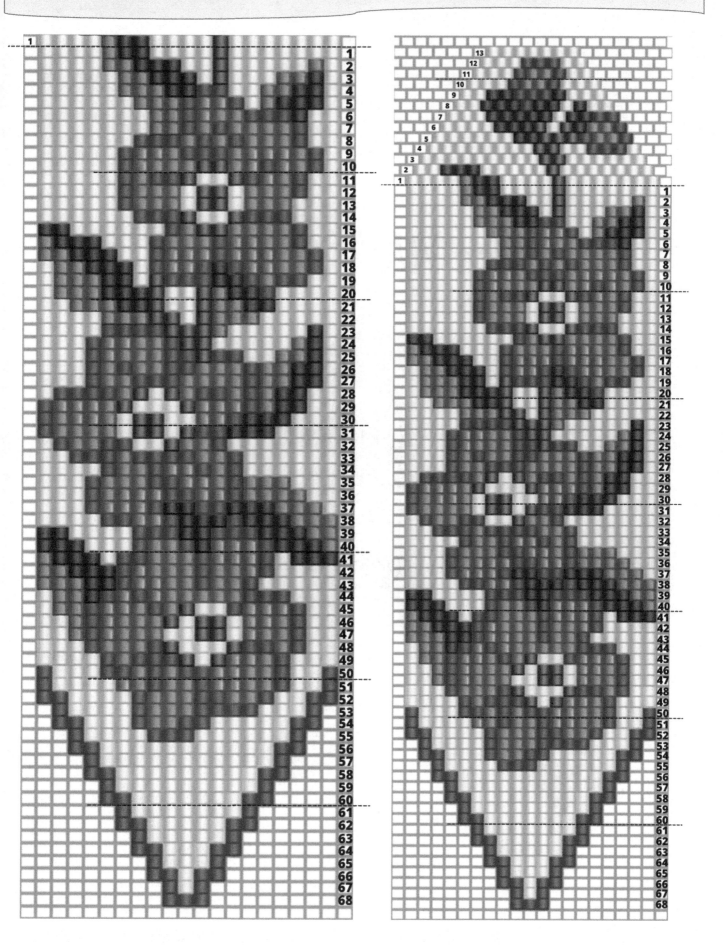

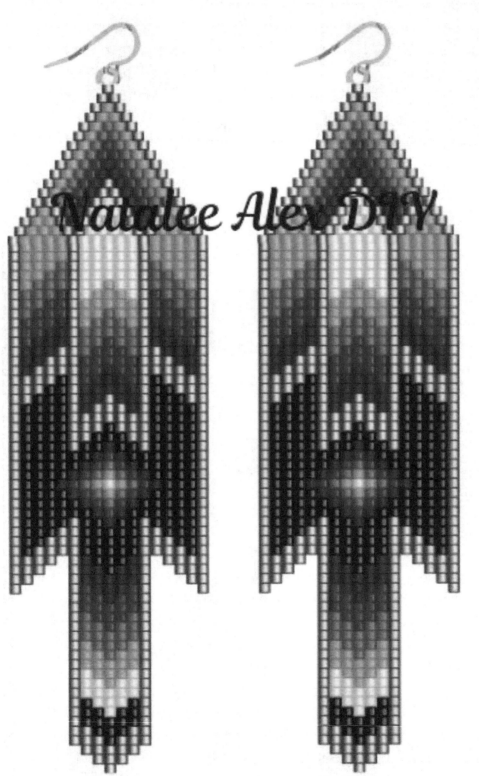

Bead List

	DB-34	24kt Gold Light Plated
		Count: 286
	DB-703	Transparent Orange
		Count: 89
	DB-722	Opaque Orange
		Count: 85
	DB-683	Frosted Silver Lined Red O
		Count: 85
	DB-378	Matte Metallic Brick Red
		Count: 85
	DB-721	Opaque Yellow
		Count: 52
	DB-10	Black
		Count: 184

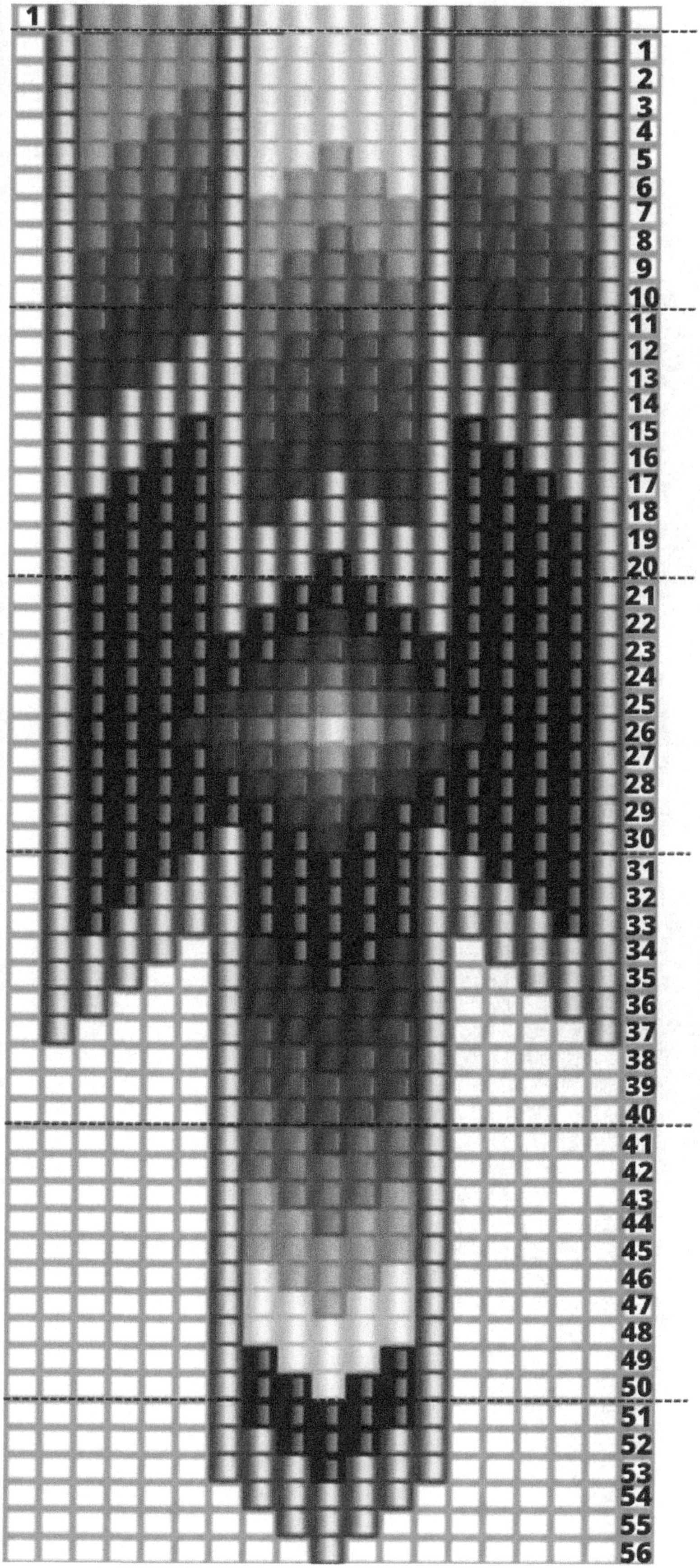

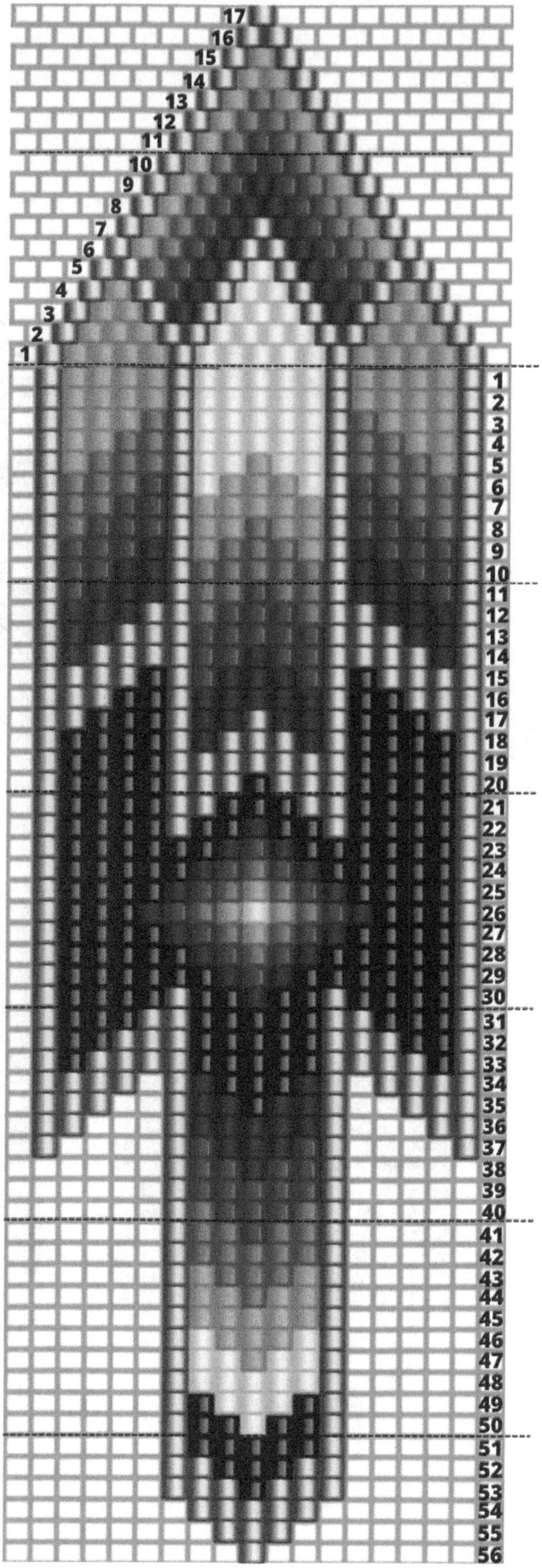

Bead List

	DB-34	
	24kt Gold Light Plated	
	Count: 405	

	DB-797	
	Frosted Opaque Jade Gree	
	Count: 211	

	DB-2261	
	Black Picasso	
	Count: 564	

	DB-2283	
	Matte Opaque Glazed Citro	
	Count: 220	

	DB-724	
	Opaque Green	
	Count: 350	

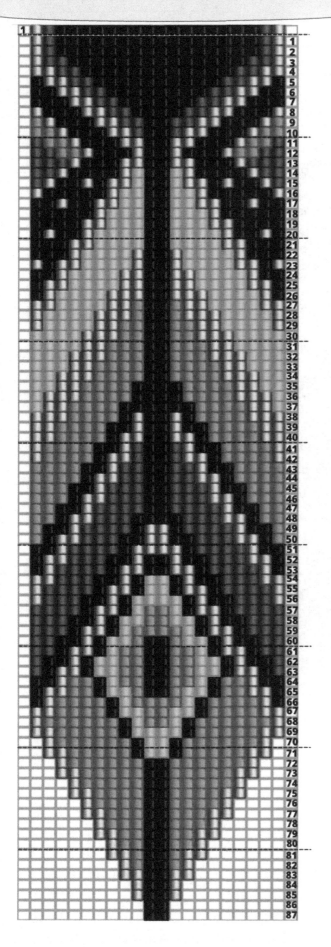

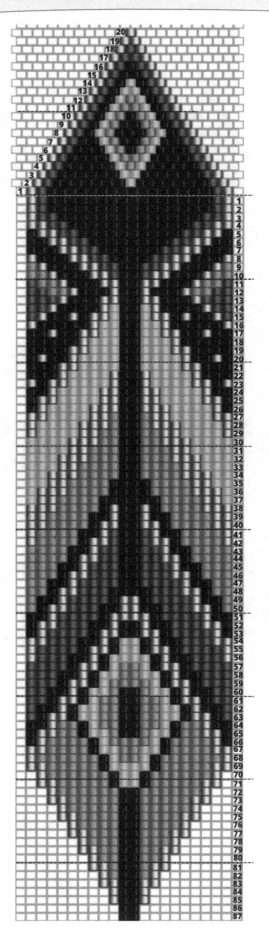

Bead List

◼	**DB-2261** Black Picasso Count: 731	
◻	**DB-34** 24kt Gold Light Plated Count: 411	
◼	**DB-797** Frosted Opaque Jade Gree Count: 68	
◼	**DB-724** Opaque Green Count: 49	
◻	**DB-721** Opaque Yellow Count: 37	
◻	**DB-50** Crystal Luster Count: 148	
◼	**DB-2283** Matte Opaque Glazed Citro Count: 23	

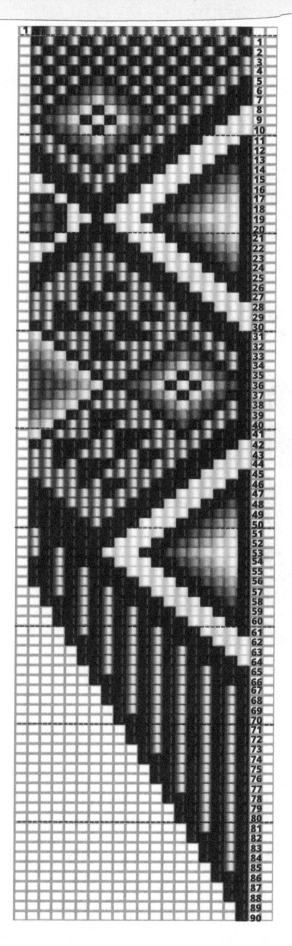

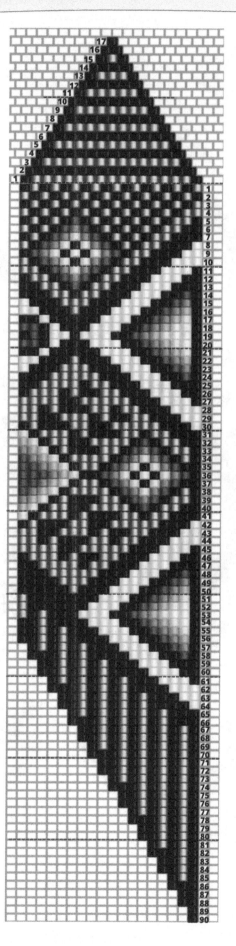

Bead List

DB-35
Galvanized Silver
Count: 288

DB-50
Crystal Luster
Count: 721

DB-465
Galvanized Midnight Blue
Count: 241

DB-714
Transparent Capri Blue
Count: 139

DB-545
Silver Blue Gold AB Palladi
Count: 140

DB-696
Frosted Silver Lined Dark E
Count: 22

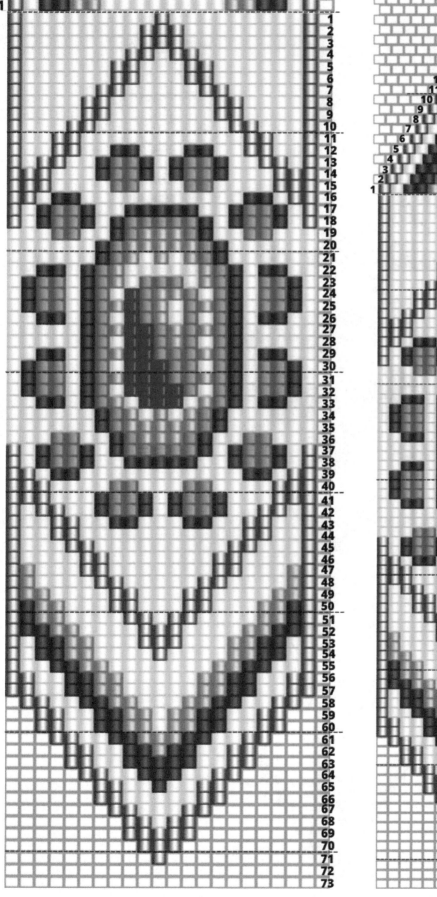

Bead List

DB-10
Black
Count: 692

DB-1182
Galvanized Frosted Dark M
Count: 264

DB-2188
Frosted Silver Lined Spear
Count: 329

DB-50
Crystal Luster
Count: 711

DB-757
Matte Opaque Vermillion R
Count: 50

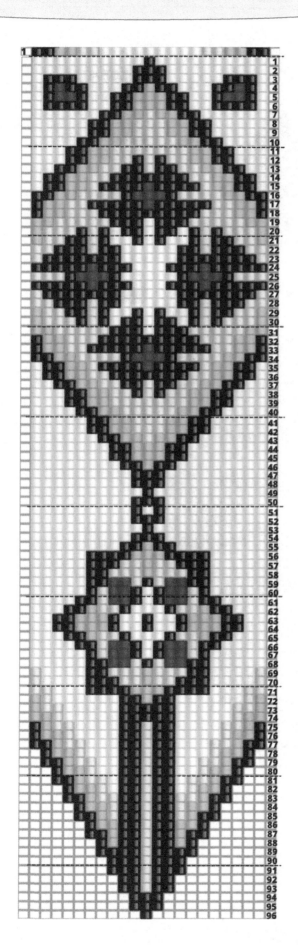

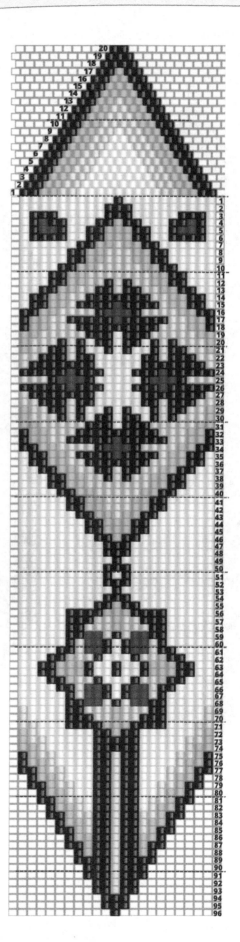

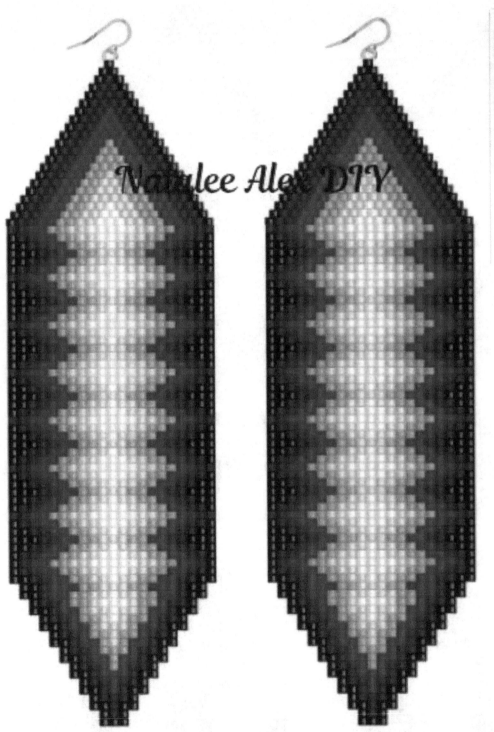

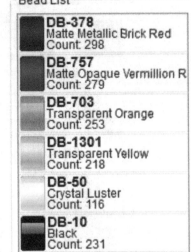

Bead List

	DB-378 Matte Metallic Brick Red Count: 298
	DB-757 Matte Opaque Vermillion R Count: 279
	DB-703 Transparent Orange Count: 253
	DB-1301 Transparent Yellow Count: 218
	DB-50 Crystal Luster Count: 116
	DB-10 Black Count: 231

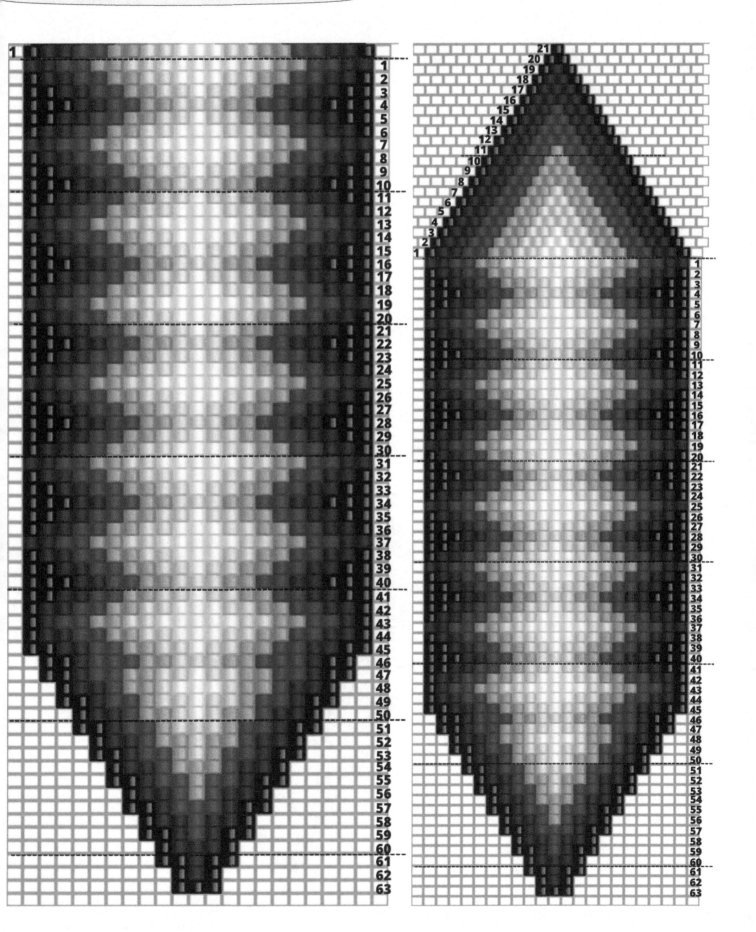

Bead List

DB-1675
Pearl Lined Pale Green Mis
Count: 410

DB-2040
Neon Mint Green
Count: 102

DB-724
Opaque Green
Count: 169

DB-797
Frosted Opaque Jade Gree
Count: 359

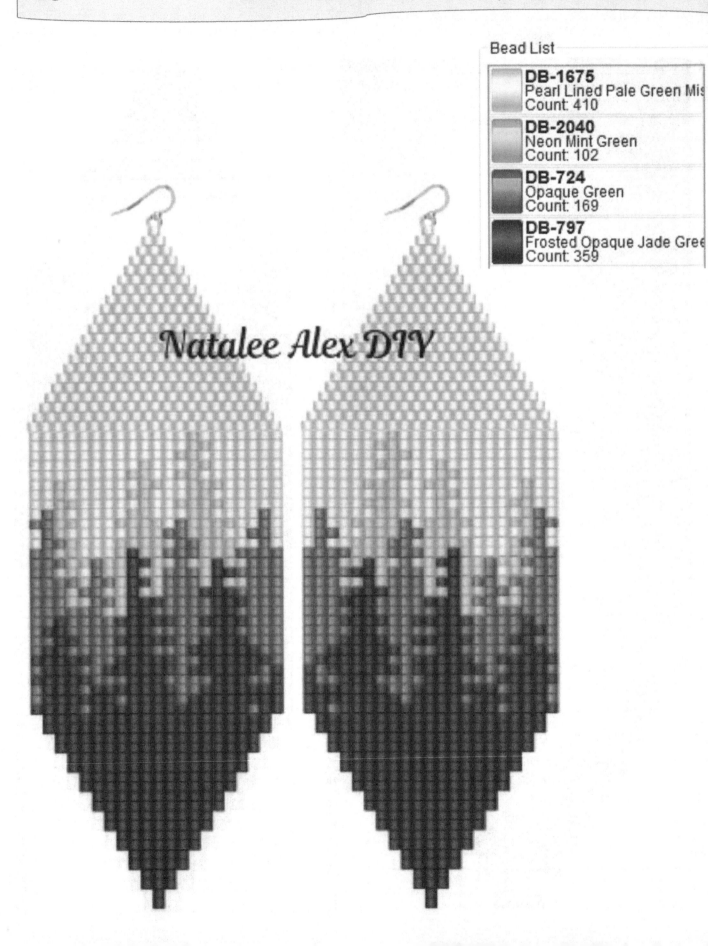

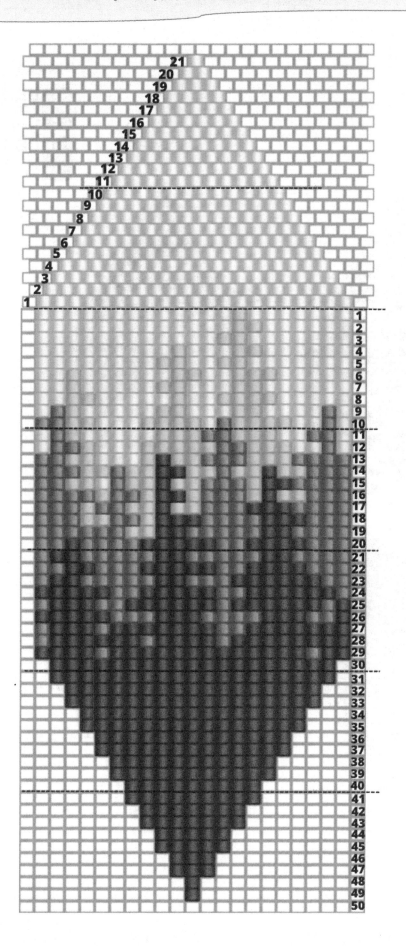

Bead List

	DB-34	24kt Gold Light Plated	Count: 427
	DB-797	Frosted Opaque Jade Gree	Count: 814
	DB-50	Crystal Luster	Count: 195

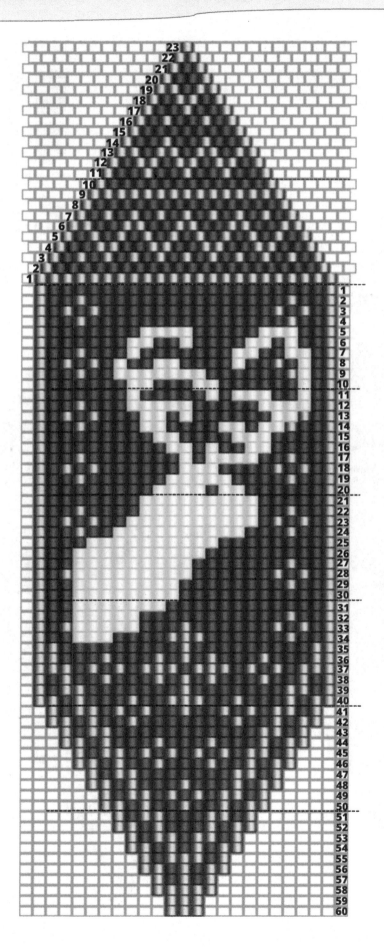

Bead List

DB-10
Black
Count: 710

DB-764
Matte Transparent Dark To|
Count: 782

DB-331
Matte 24kt Gold Plated
Count: 148

DB-771
Frosted Transparent Saffro
Count: 154

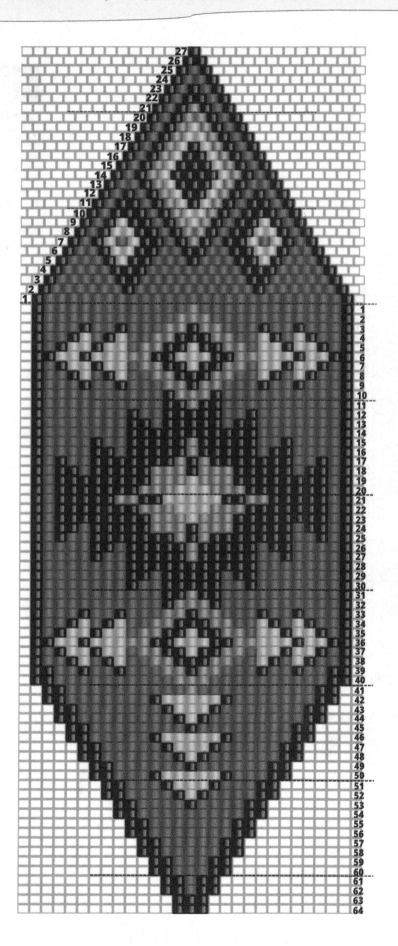

Bead List

	DB-10	Black	Count: 644
	DB-764	Matte Transparent Dark To	Count: 466
	DB-331	Matte 24kt Gold Plated	Count: 340
	DB-149	Silver Lined Capri Blue	Count: 254
	DB-164	Opaque Turquoise Blue AB	Count: 35

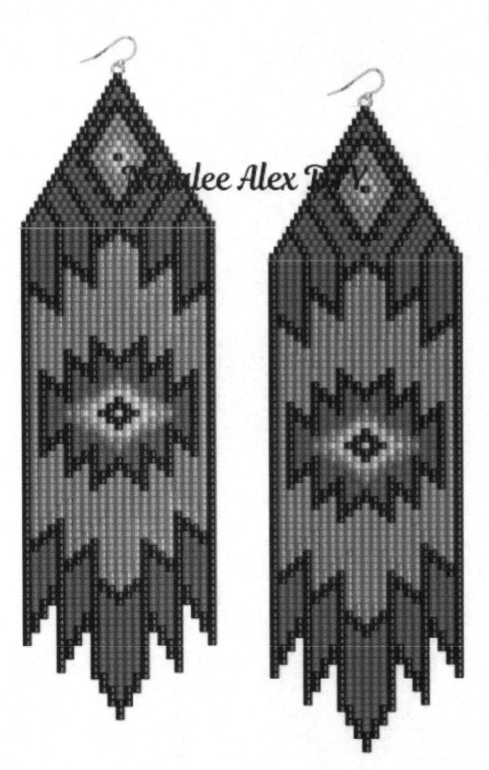

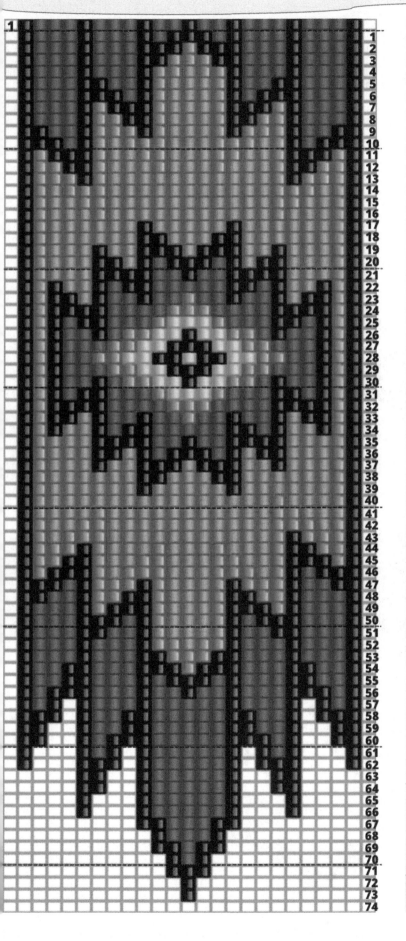

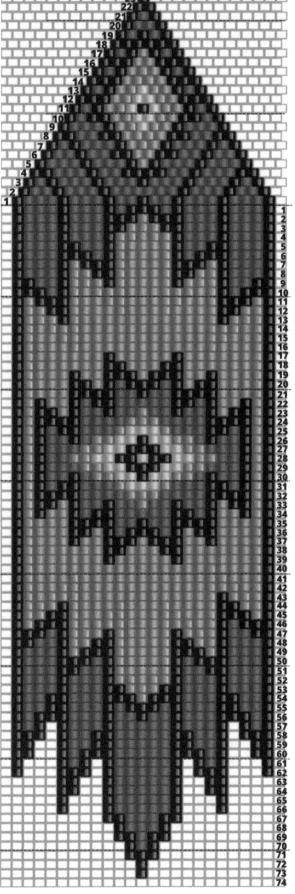

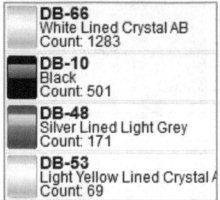

Bead List

DB-66
White Lined Crystal AB
Count: 1283

DB-10
Black
Count: 501

DB-48
Silver Lined Light Grey
Count: 171

DB-53
Light Yellow Lined Crystal A
Count: 69

DB-45
Silver Lined Orange
Count: 144

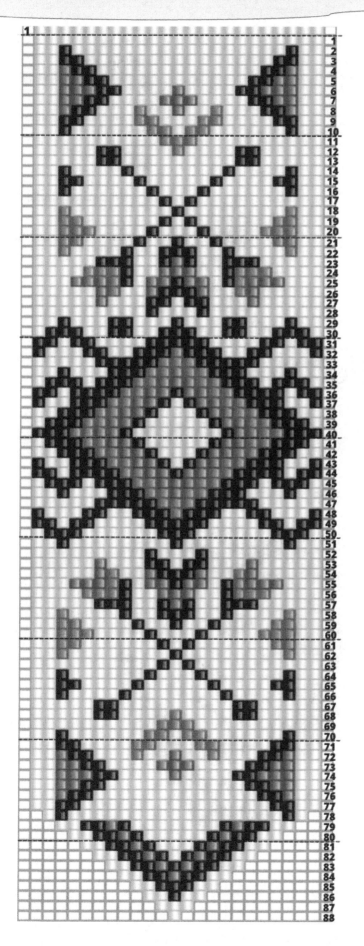

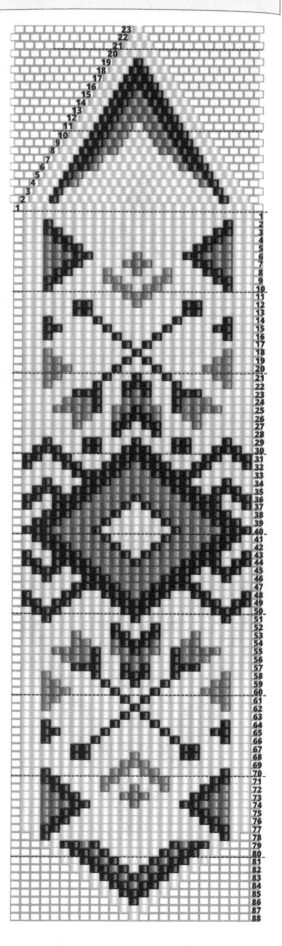

Bead List

DB-45
Silver Lined Orange
Count: 187

DB-48
Silver Lined Light Grey
Count: 261

DB-10
Black
Count: 292

DB-66
White Lined Crystal AB
Count: 1231

DB-53
Light Yellow Lined Crystal A
Count: 40

Bead List

	DB-10	Black	Count: 424
	DB-45	Silver Lined Orange	Count: 522
	DB-53	Light Yellow Lined Crystal A	Count: 281

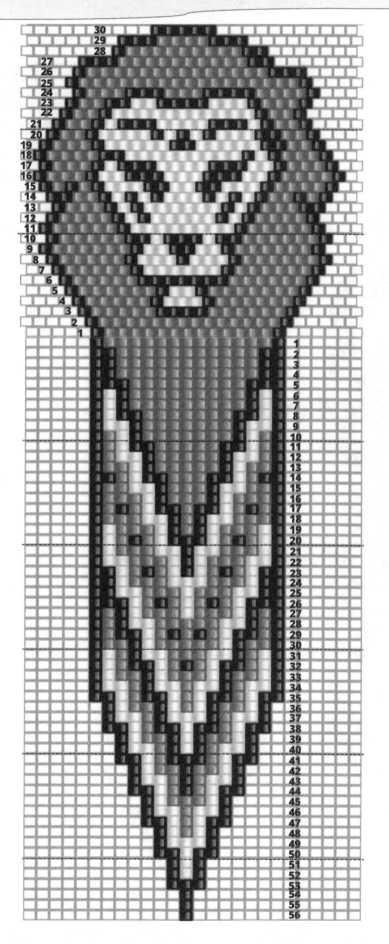

Bead List

DB-751
Matte Opaque Yellow
Count: 353

DB-704
Transparent Red Orange
Count: 195

DB-797
Frosted Opaque Jade Gree
Count: 342

DB-1474
Transparent Pale Green Mi
Count: 602

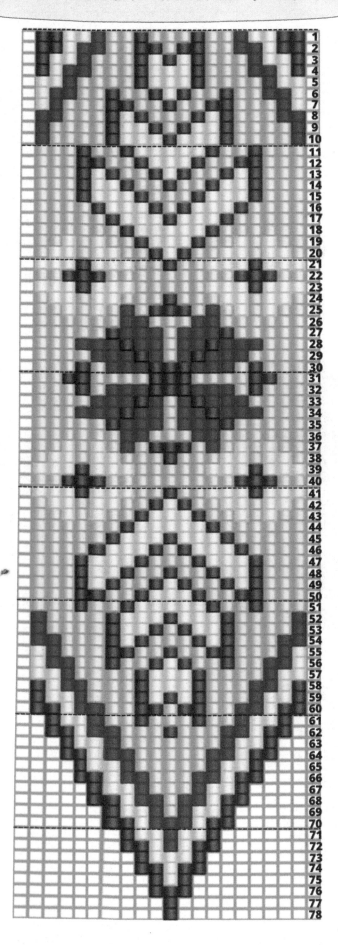

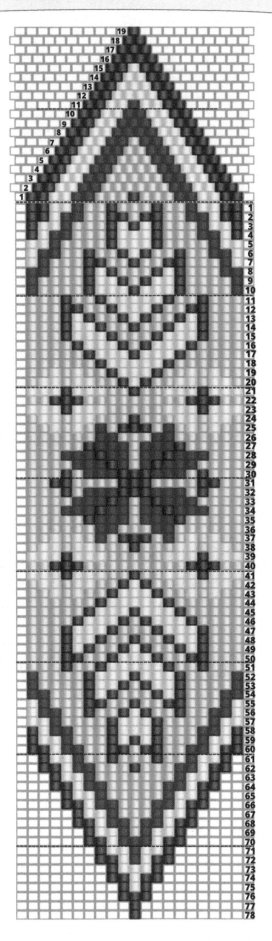

Bead List

DB-10
Black
Count: 793

DB-45
Silver Lined Orange
Count: 159

DB-44
Silver Lined Aqua
Count: 166

DB-34
24kt Gold Light Plated
Count: 386

DB-704
Transparent Red Orange
Count: 201

DB-1315
Transparent Red Violet
Count: 154

DB-50
Crystal Luster
Count: 395

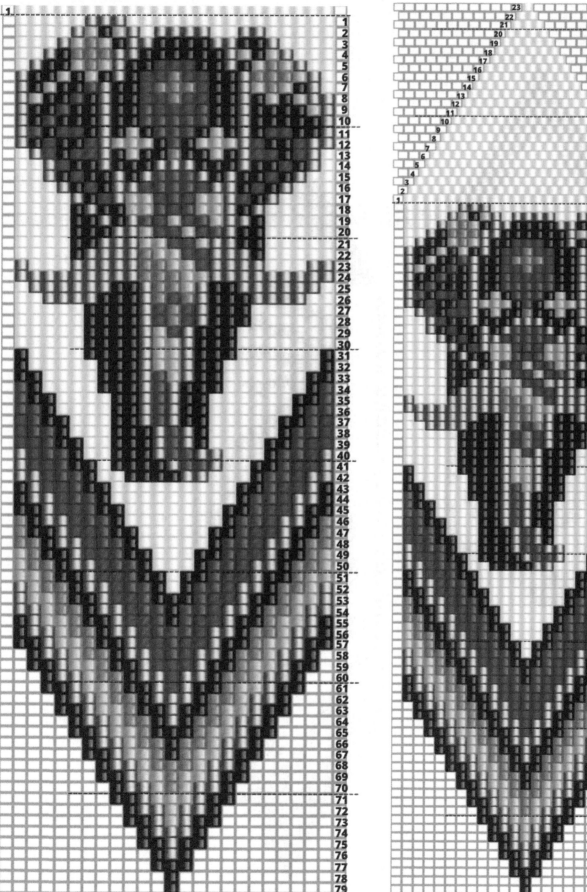

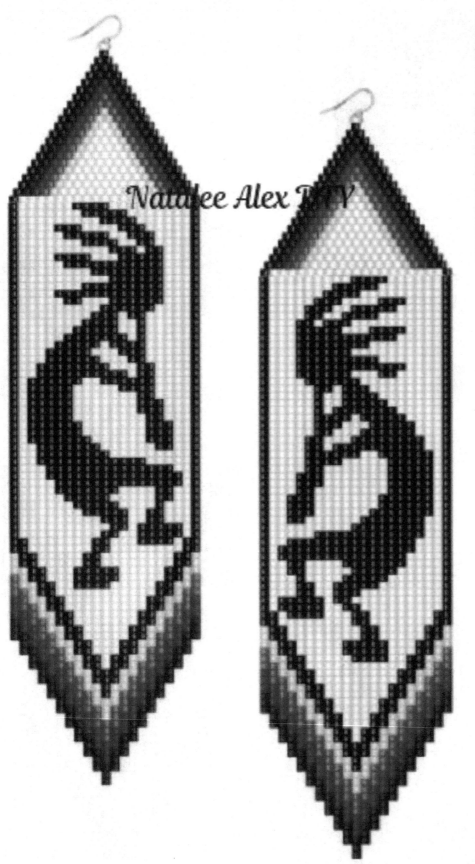

Bead List

DB-10
Black
Count: 616

DB-50
Crystal Luster
Count: 707

DB-743
Matte Transparent Yellow
Count: 86

DB-682
Frosted Silver Lined Dark (
Count: 90

DB-683
Frosted Silver Lined Red O
Count: 94

DB-2263
Opaque Red Picasso
Count: 98

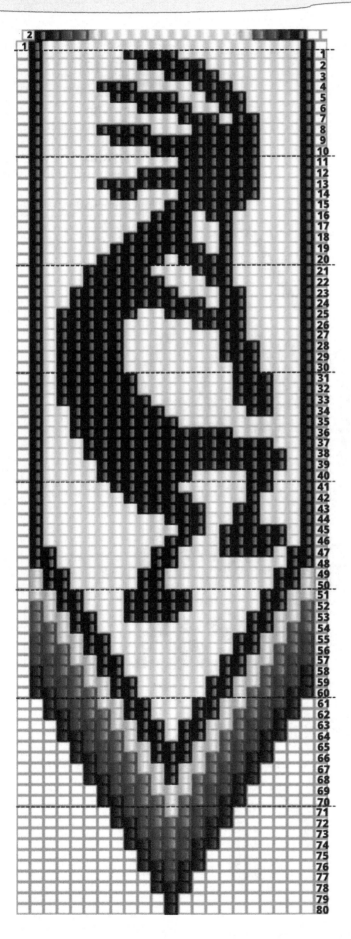

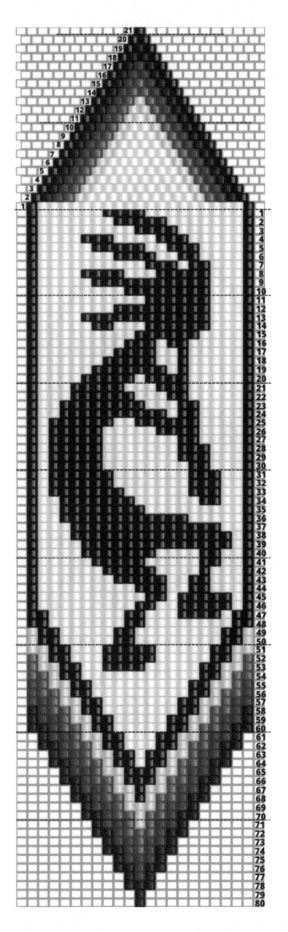

Natalee Alex DIY

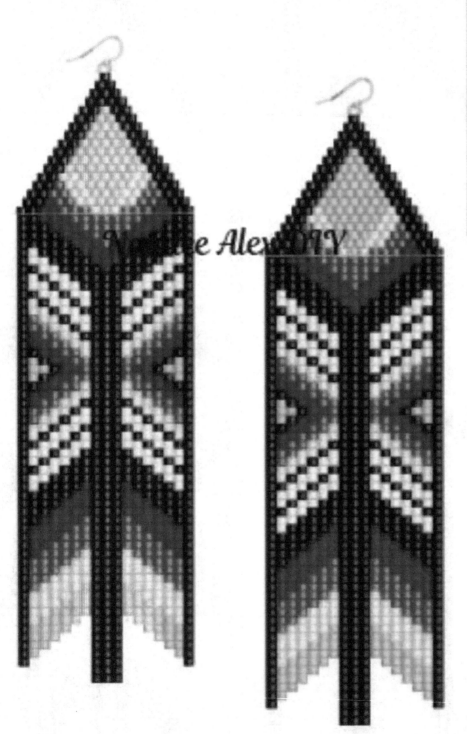

Bead List

DB-10
Black
Count: 473

DB-658
Opaque Turquoise Green
Count: 105

DB-751
Matte Opaque Yellow
Count: 116

DB-161
Opaque Orange AB
Count: 127

DB-727
Opaque Vermillion Red
Count: 118

DB-50
Crystal Luster
Count: 96

Bead List

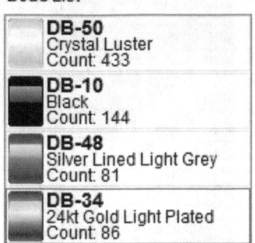

DB-50
Crystal Luster
Count: 433

DB-10
Black
Count: 144

DB-48
Silver Lined Light Grey
Count: 81

DB-34
24kt Gold Light Plated
Count: 86

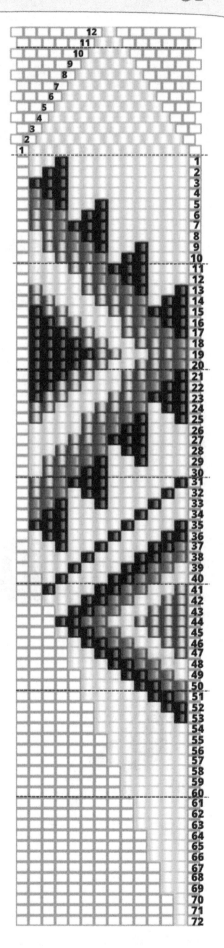

CREATE YOUR OWN DESIGN

Name project _____

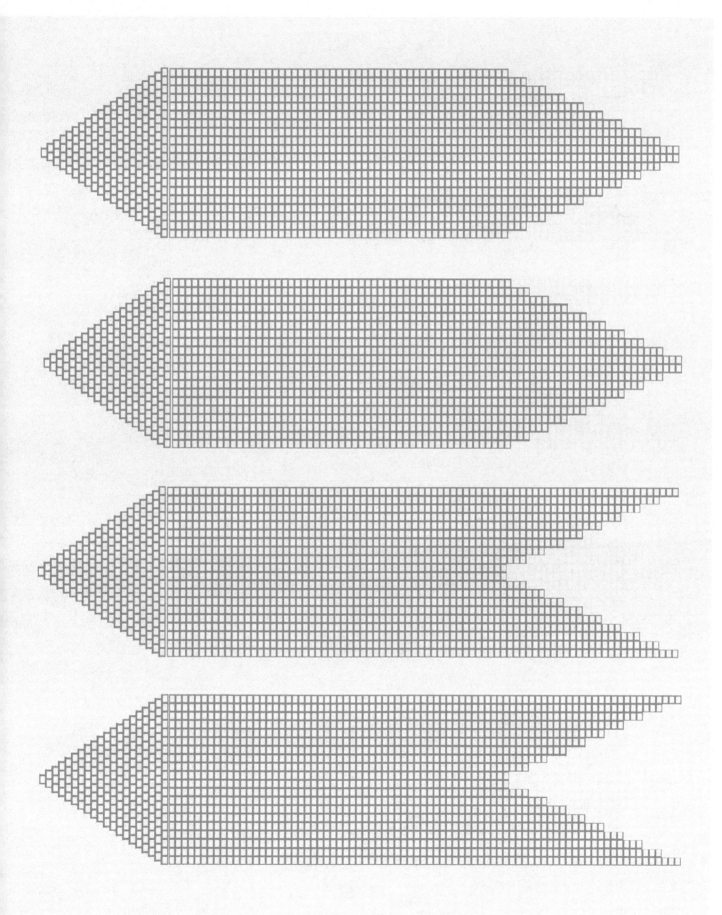

Name project _____

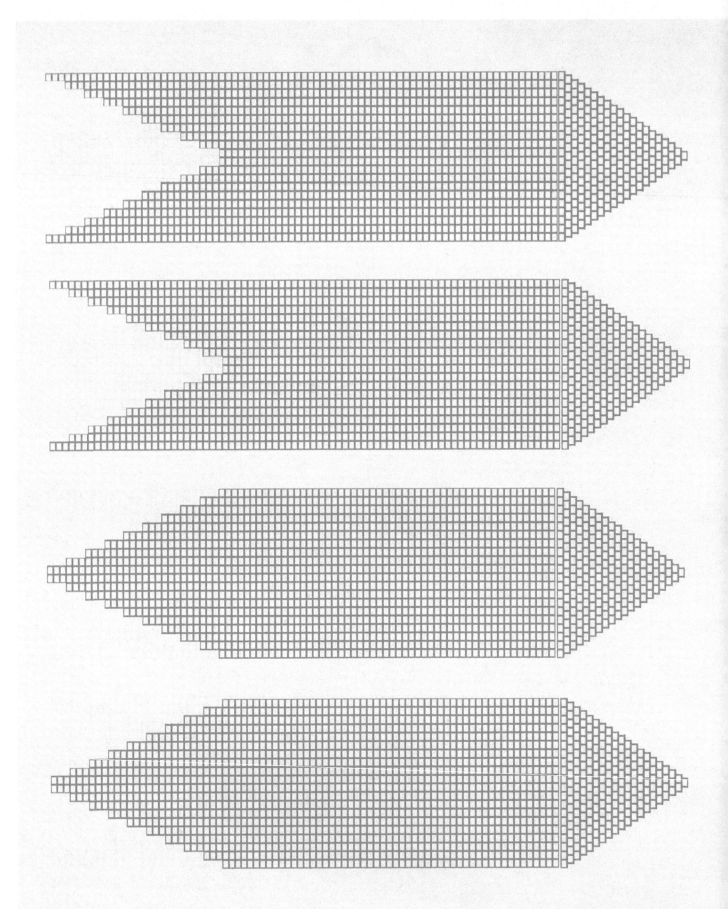

Name project _____

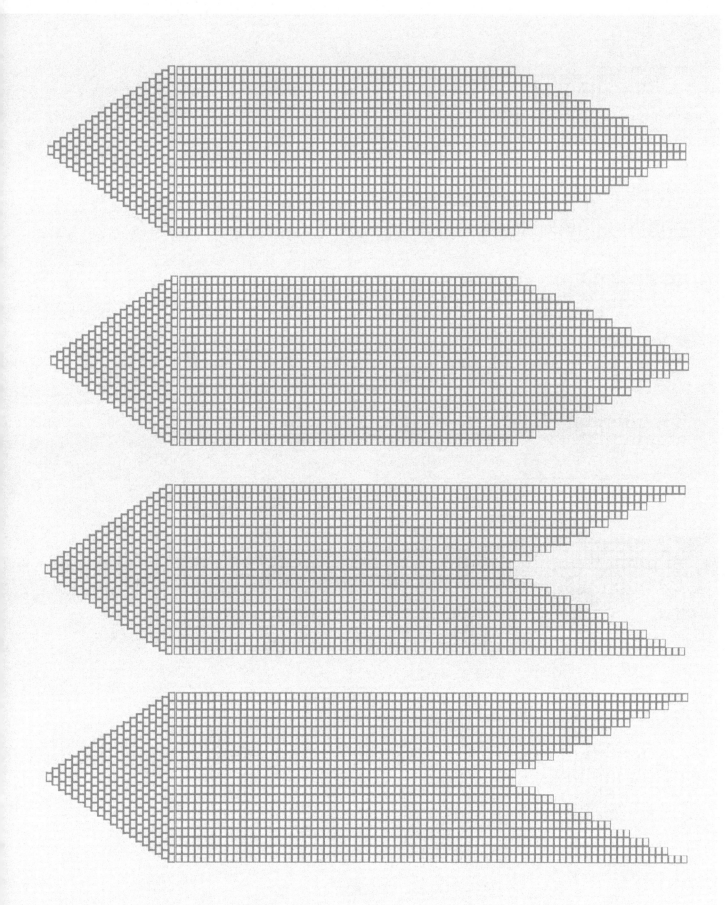

Name project _____

Name project _____

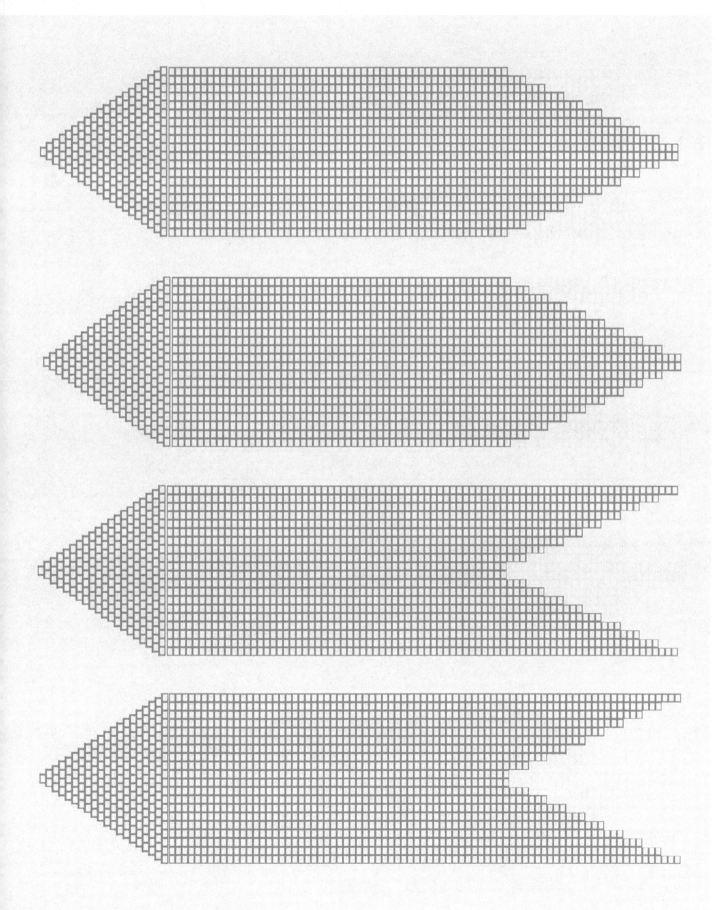

Name project _____

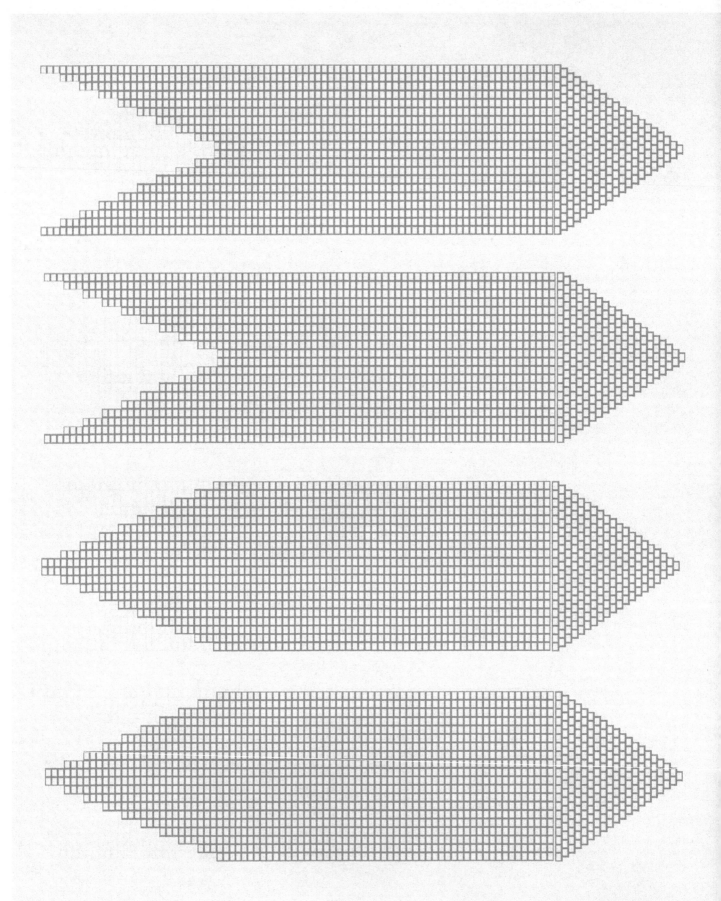

Name project _____

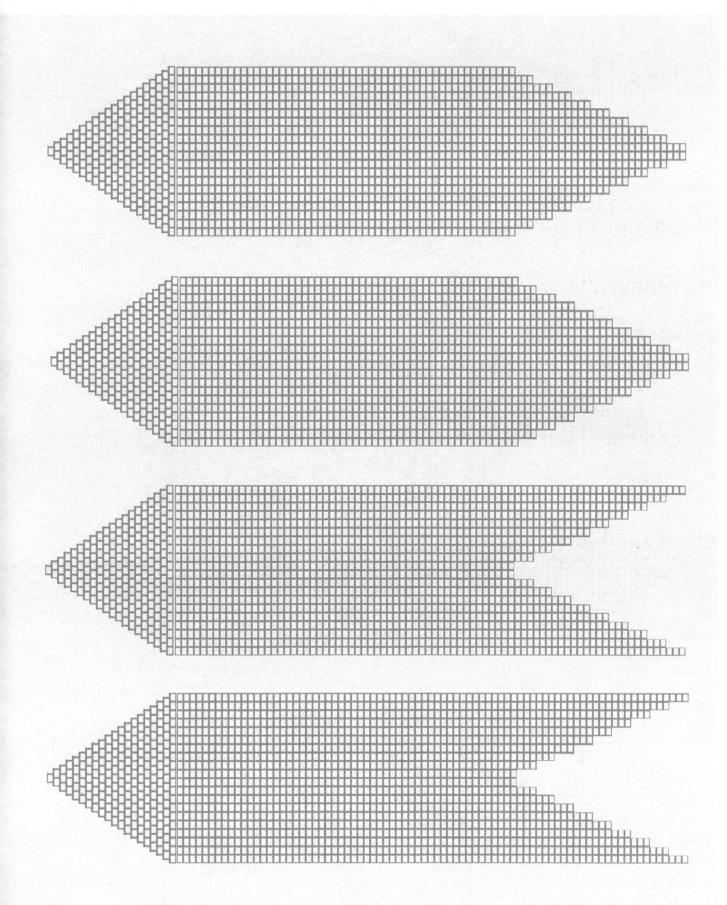

Name project _____

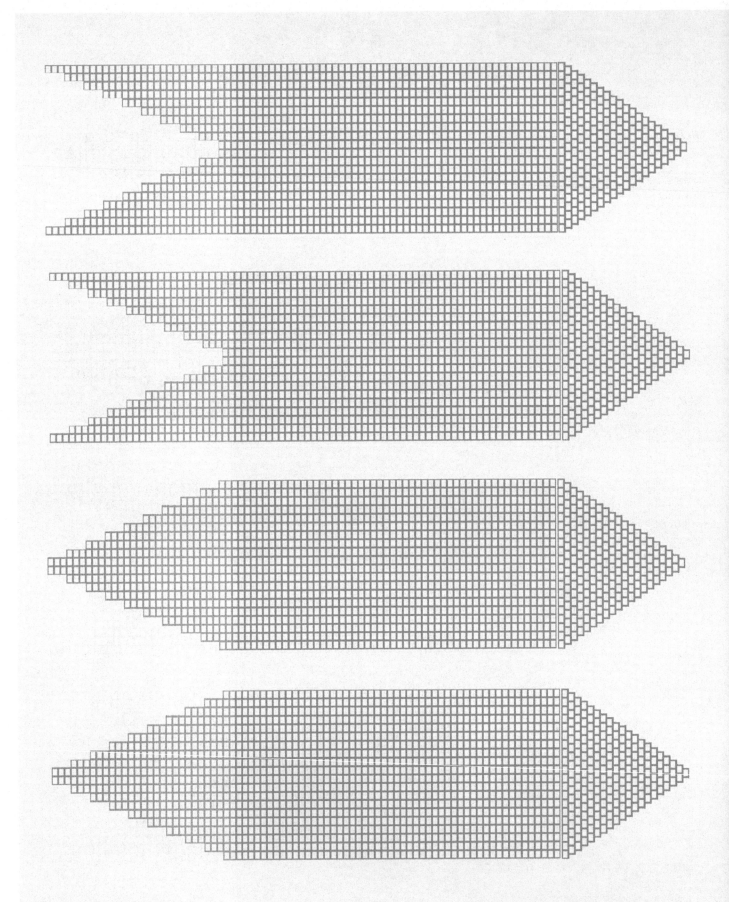

Name project _____

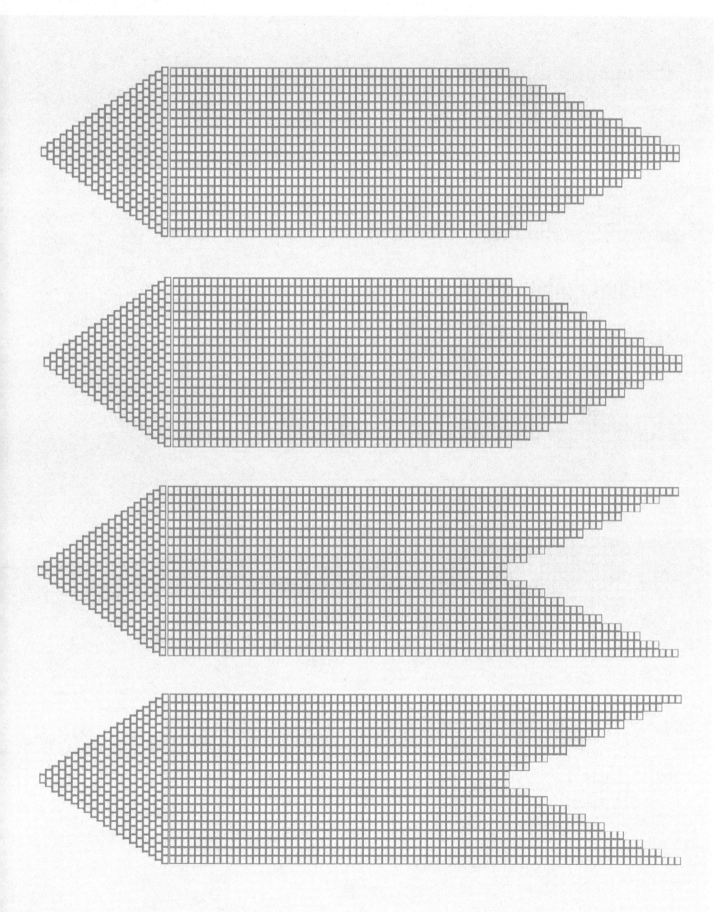

Name project _____

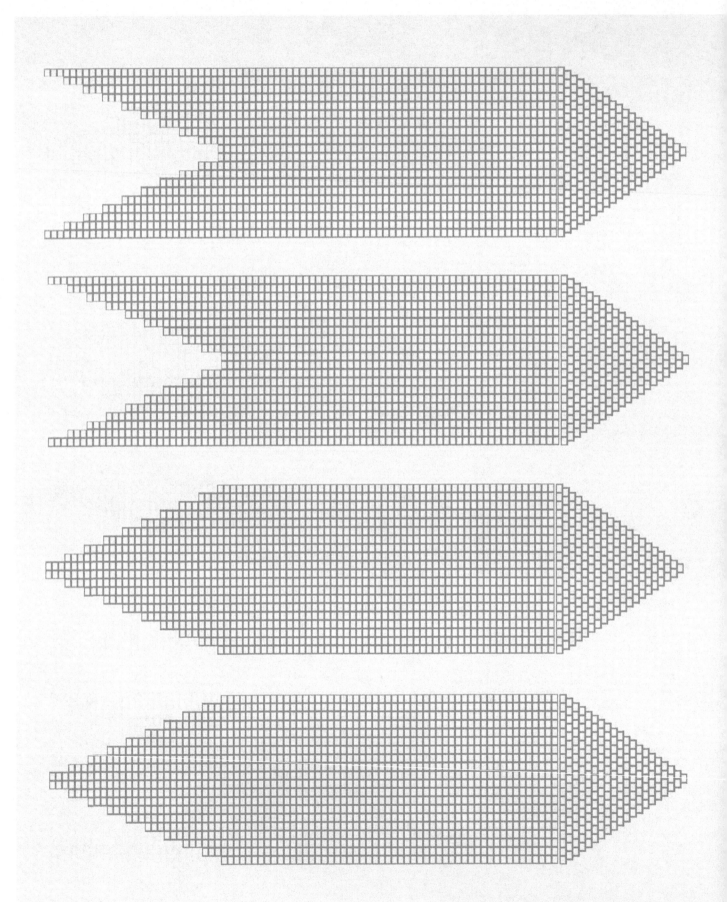

Name project _____

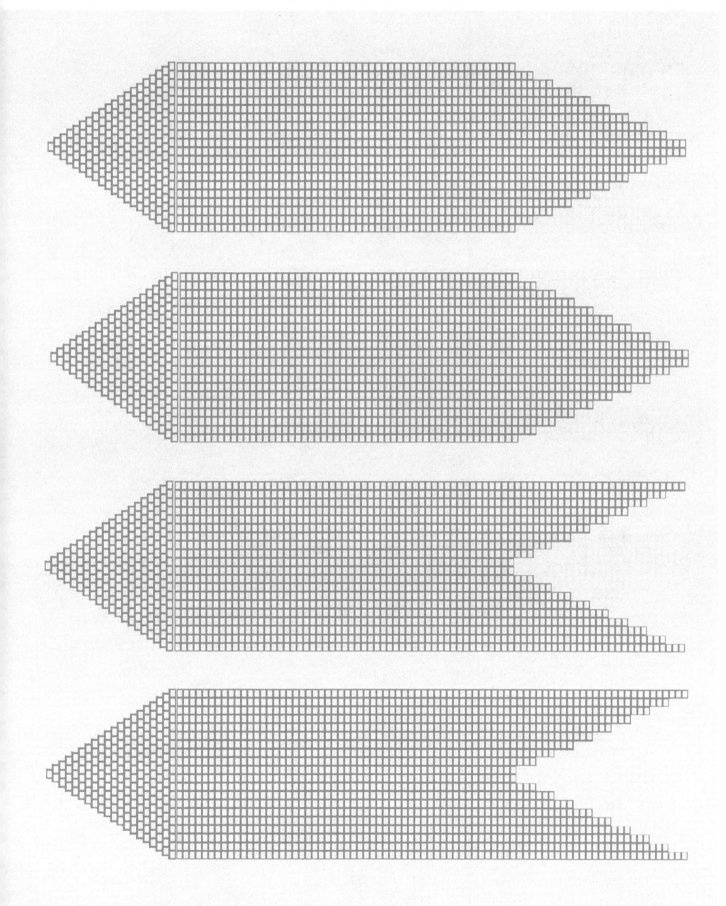

Name project _____

Name project _____

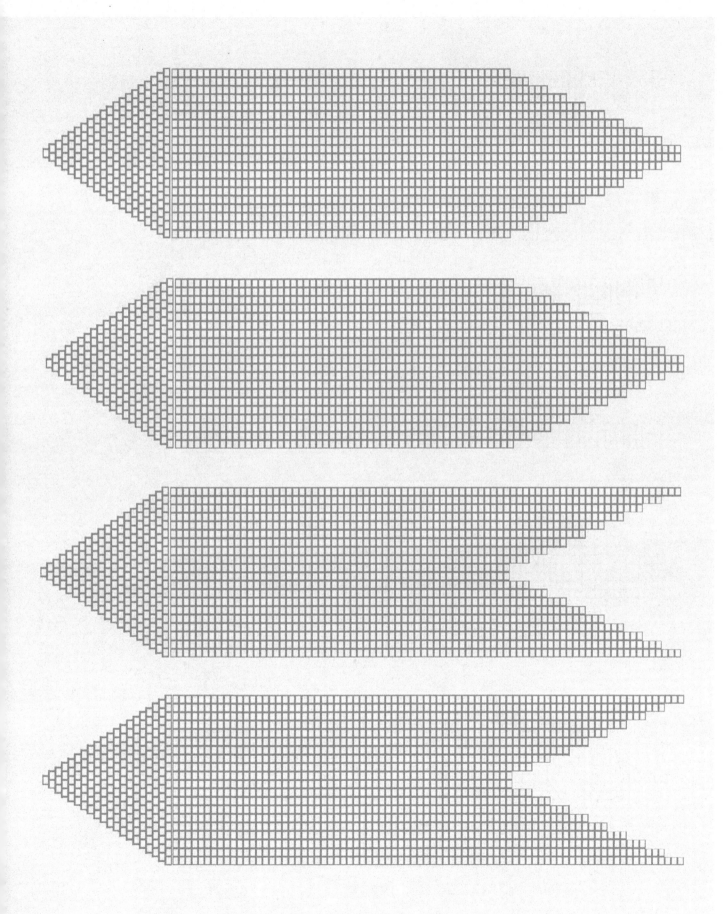

Name project _____

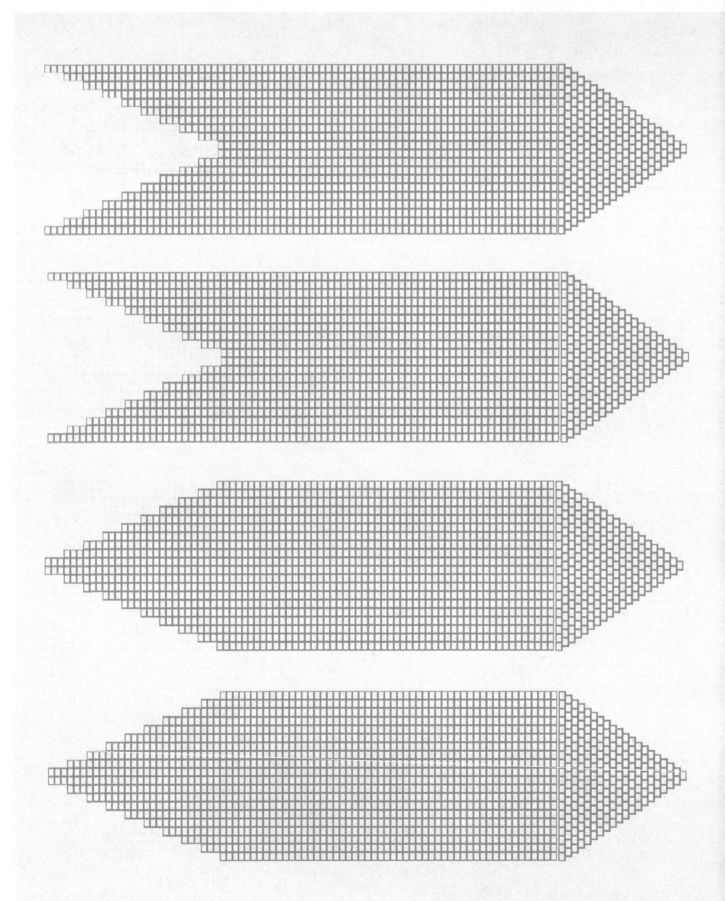

Name project _____

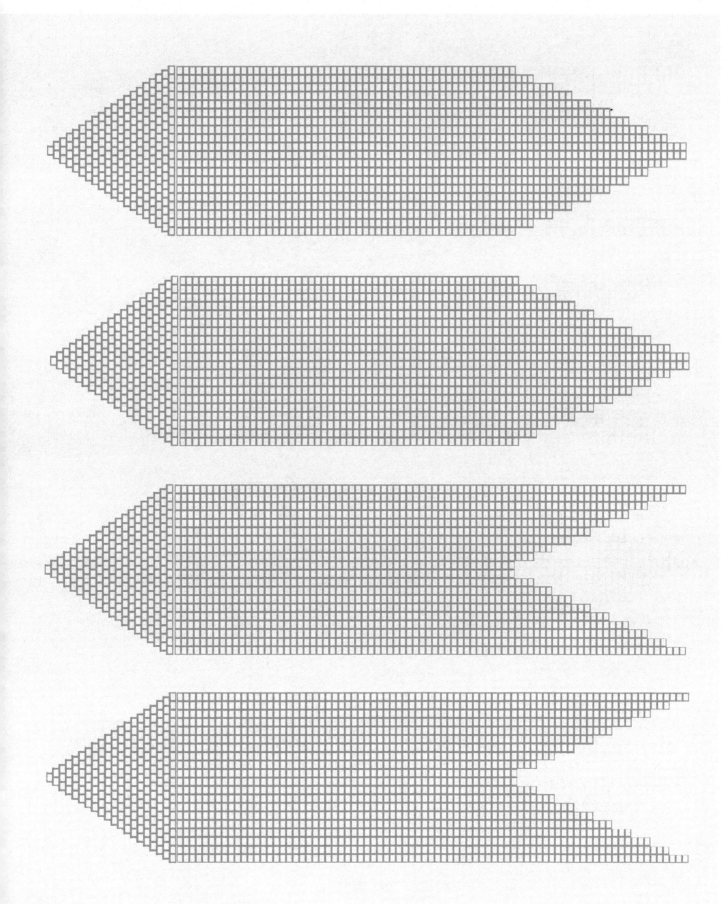

Name project _____

Name project _____

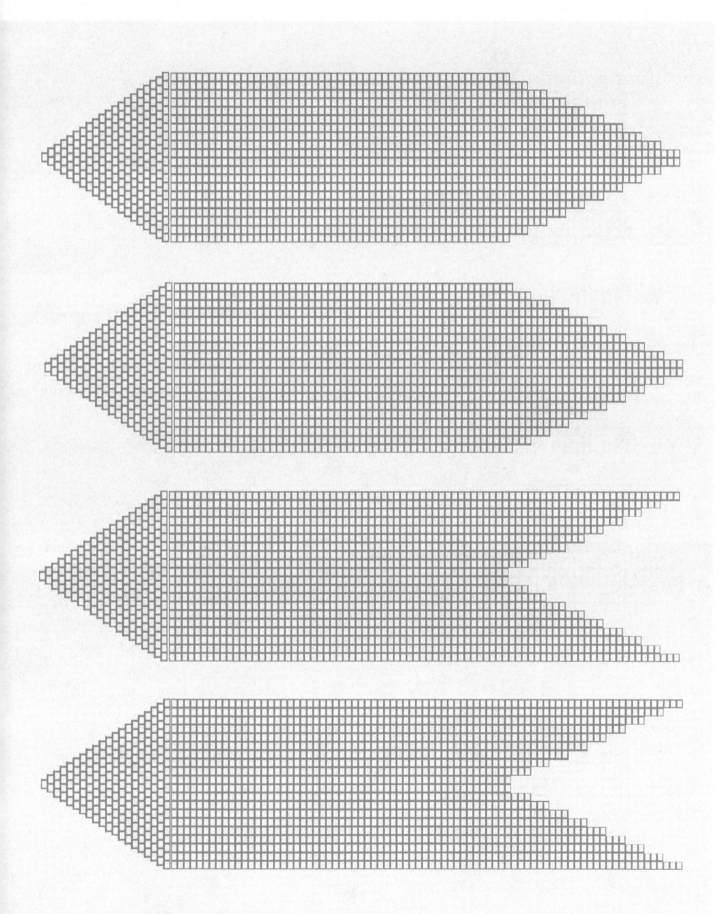

Name project _____

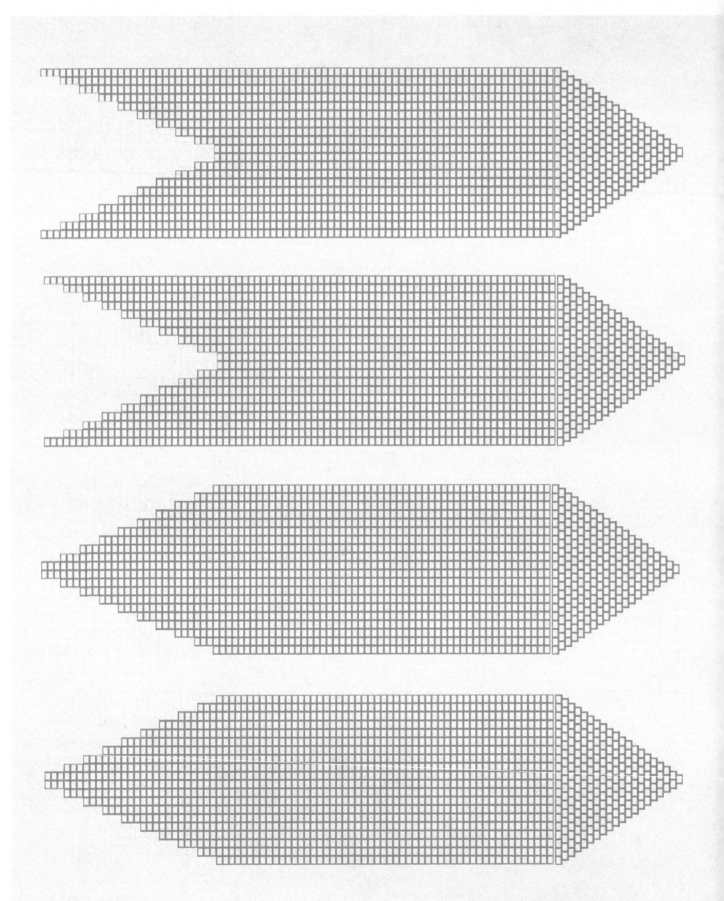

Name project _____

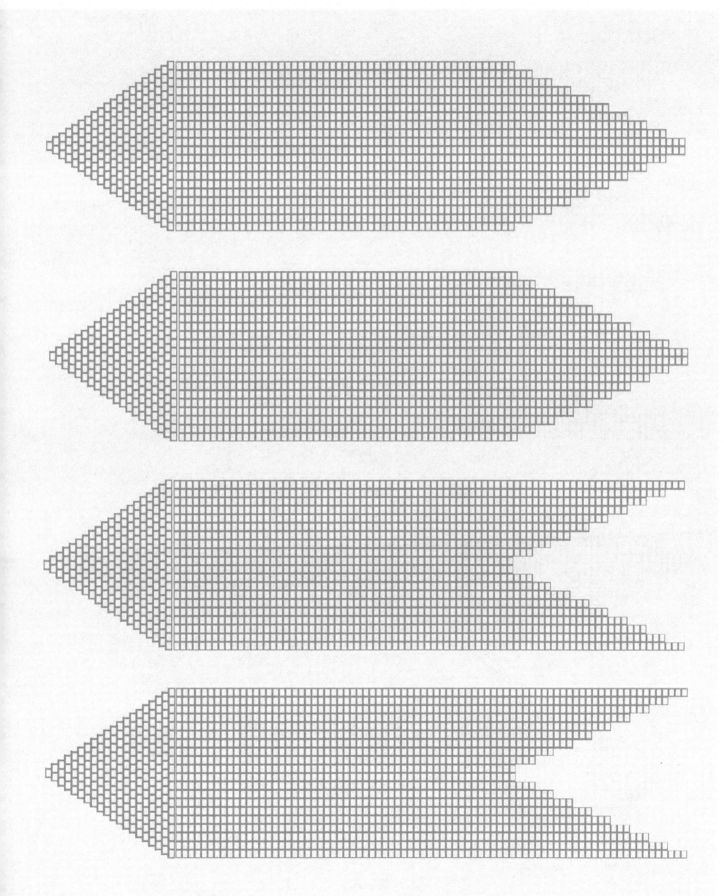

Name project _____

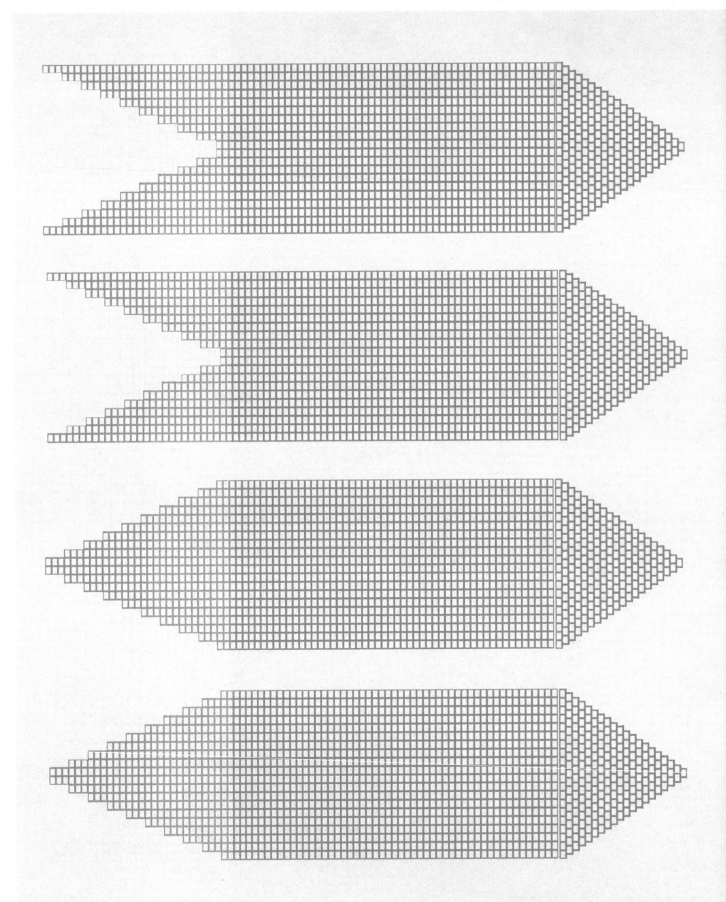

Name project _____

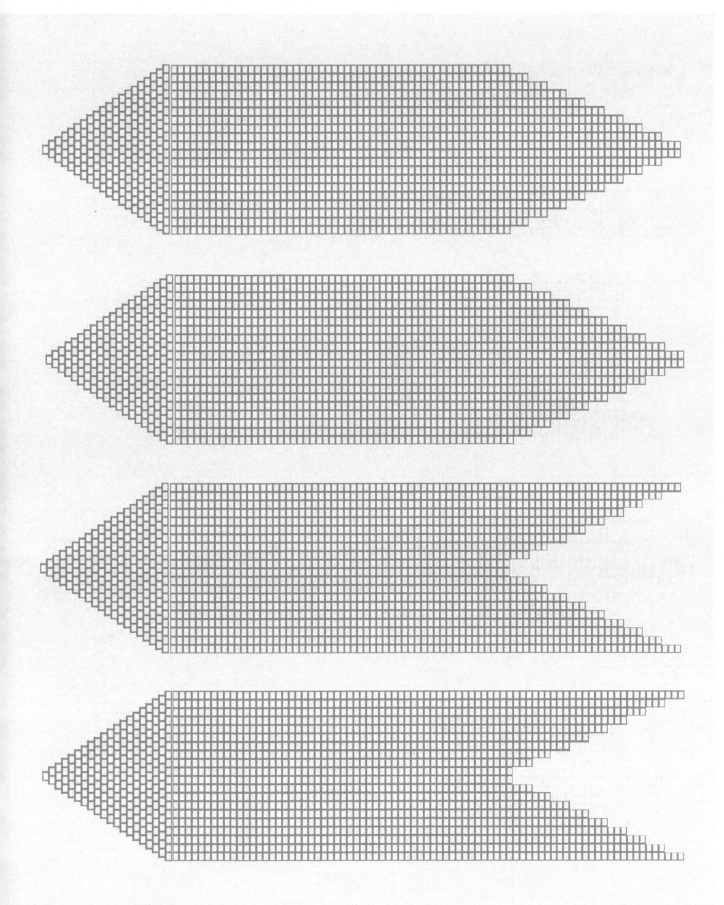

Name project _____

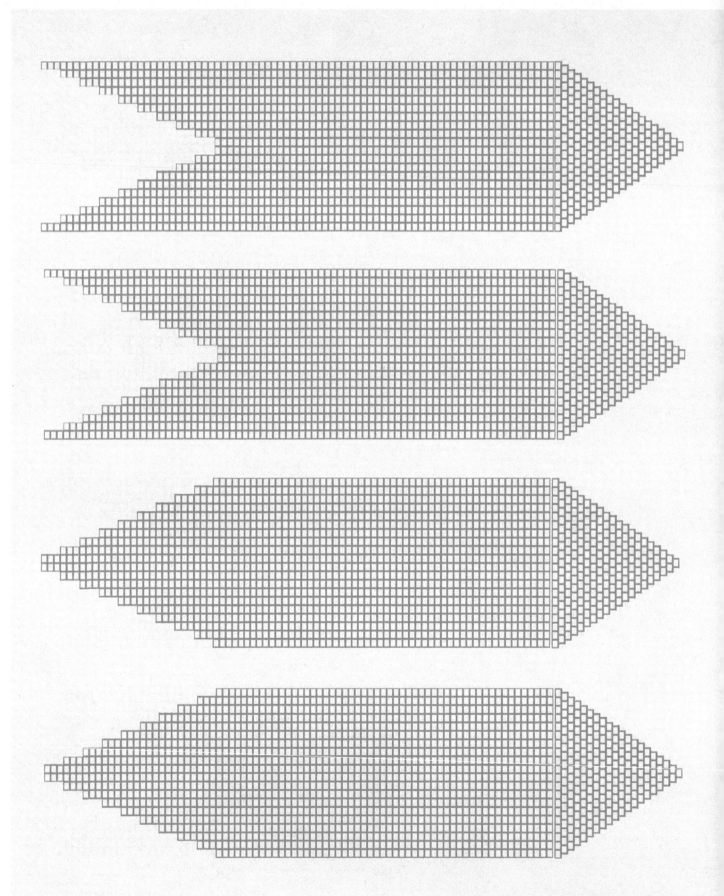

Name project _____

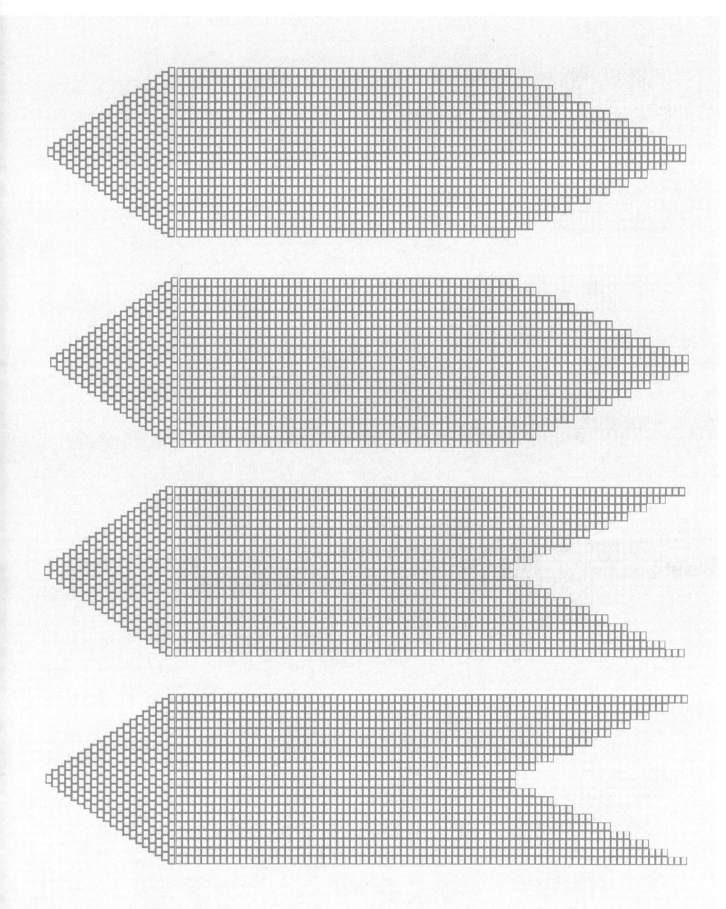

Name project _____

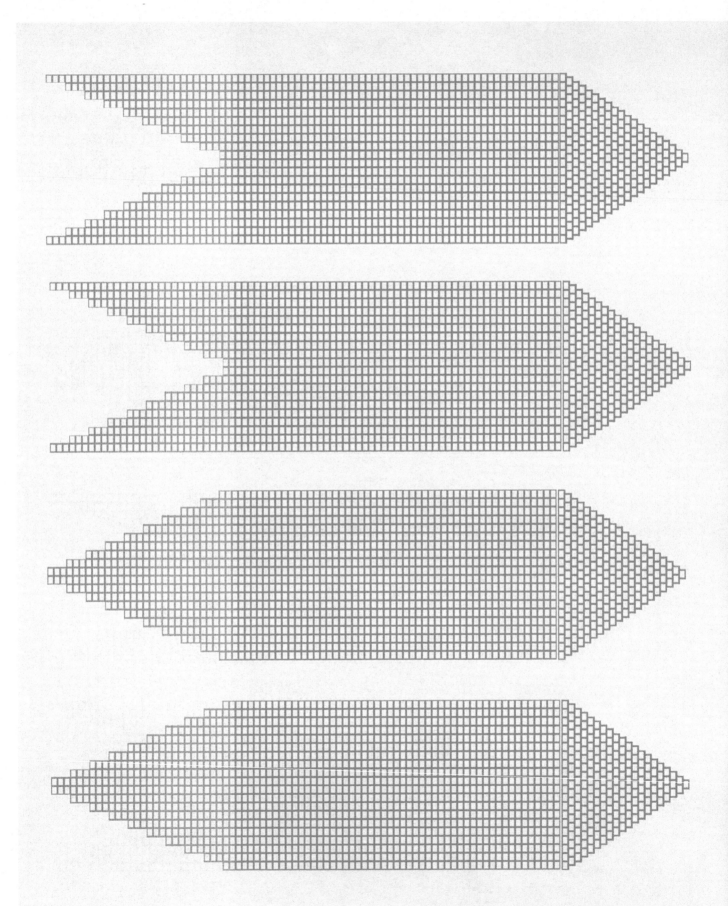

BRICK STITCH PATTERNS
by Natalee Alex

24 projects

SEED BEAD EARRINGS FRINGE

BEADING PATTERNS

PAYOTE PATTERNS
by Natalee Alex

24 projects

SEED BEAD BRACELETS

BEADING PATTERNS

BRICK STITCH PATTERNS
by Natalee Alex

24

SEED BEAD EARRINGS TEARDROP

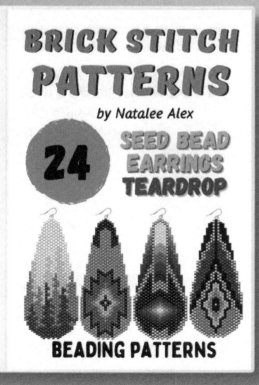

BEADING PATTERNS

BRICK STITCH PATTERNS
by Natalee Alex

24

SEED BEAD EARRINGS

BEADING PATTERNS

HOW TO STITCH 3D PEYOTE STAR

15 PROJECTS

Tutorial for beginners

HOW TO STITCH 3D PEYOTE STAR

15 PROJECTS

Tutorial for beginners

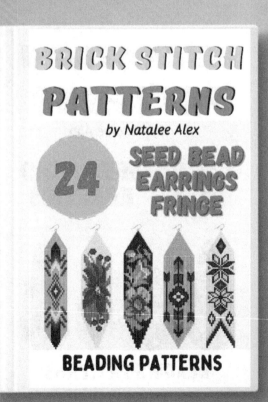

BRICK STITCH PATTERNS

by Natalee Alex

24 SEED BEAD EARRINGS FRINGE

BEADING PATTERNS

BRICK STITCH PATTERNS

by Natalee Alex

24 projects SEED BEAD EARRINGS FRINGE

NATIVE AMERICAN STYLE

See more books on my Amazon Author Page
https://www.amazon.com/author/nataleealex

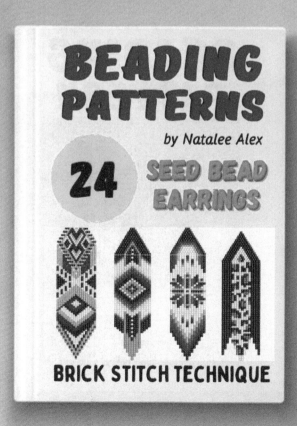

See more books on my Amazon Author Page
https://www.amazon.com/author/nataleealex

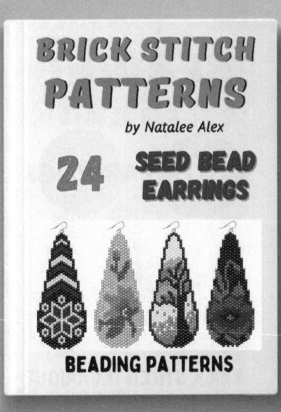

Made in the USA
Coppell, TX
10 February 2024

28799610R20046